The IT PMO Career

A Roadmap Through To Management

Mark Readman

Copyright © 2015 Mark Readman

All rights reserved.

No part of this publication may be reproduced, stored in a retrieval system, or transmitted in any form or by any means without the prior permission in writing of the publisher. Nor be otherwise circulated in any form of binding or cover other than that in which it is published and without a similar condition including this condition being imposed on the subsequent purchaser.

The purpose of this book is to educate and provide information on the subject matter covered. All attempts have been made to verify the information at the time of publication, and the author does not assume any responsibility for errors, omissions or other interpretations of the subject matter. The purchaser or reader of this book assumes responsibility of the use of this material and information. The author assumes no responsibility or liability on behalf of any purchaser or reader of this book.

ISBN-13: 978-1511921039
ISBN-10: 151192103X

"I wanted to write a book that helps the PMO professional understand where their knowledge levels are, how to become the best they can be in their current role and also demonstrate what is required to reach the next stage of the PMO career path."

Mark Readman

Contents

FOREWORD **9**

CHAPTER ONE: THE BEGINNING – WHAT IS A PMO? **13**
    Reality vs Textbook 13
    The PMO Resources 14
        The PMO Analyst 14
        The PMO Manager 16
        The Head of PMO\PMO Director 19

CHAPTER TWO: MEETING SUPPORT AND FACILITATION .. **21**
    Meeting Invites 21
    Room Preparation 22
    Meeting Management 22
    Minutes and Actions 23
    Meeting Tips 23

CHAPTER THREE: STATUS REPORTING **25**
    Definition 25
    The Reporting Cycle 26

Reporting – Ongoing Management **28**
    Meetings and Regular Reviews 28
    PMO Analyst Role 28
    PMO Manager's Role 28
        Process Review 28
        Programme Level Reporting 30

CHAPTER FOUR: PROJECT SCHEDULE **31**
    Definition 31
        Project Schedule vs Project Plan 31
        Reality vs Textbook 32
    The Levels of Project Schedule 32
    Resource Management 34
    PMO Analyst Role 34

    Project Schedule Assurance 36

CHAPTER FIVE: PROGRAMME SCHEDULE 39
    Definition 39
    PMO Manager's Role 39
        Process Review 40
        "At a Glance" Metrics 40

CHAPTER SIX: RISK AND ISSUE MANAGEMENT 43

Risks 43
    Definition 43
    The Risk Log (Register) 44
    Identification 46
    Description 48
    Risk Rating – Impact vs Probability Matrix 49
    Mitigation Planning 51

Issues 53
    Definition 53
    The Issue Log (Register) 53
    Identification 55
    Description 56
    Issue Rating - Priority 57
    Mitigation Planning 58

Risks and Issues – Ongoing Management 59
    Progress Updates 59
    Meetings and Regular Reviews 59
    PMO Analyst Role 60
    PMO Manager's Role 61
        Process Review 61
        "At a Glance" Metrics 63
        Address the Root Causes 64

CHAPTER SEVEN: DEPENDENCY MANAGEMENT 65
    Definition 65

The Dependency Log (Register) 65
  Identification 67
  Description 68
  Dependency Rating – Priority 68
  Mitigation Planning 69

Dependencies – Ongoing Management 70
  Meetings and Regular Reviews 70
  PMO Analyst Role 70
  PMO Manager's Role 71
    Process Review 71
    "At a Glance" Metrics 73

CHAPTER EIGHT: CHANGE CONTROL 75
  Definition 75
  Proposing a Change 76
  Change Request (CR) Form 76
  Impact Assessment 78
  The Change Control Log (Register) 78
  The Change Board (CCB) 79
  Closing a Change Request 79

Change Control – Ongoing Management 81
  PMO Analyst Role 81
  PMO Manager's Role 81
    "At a Glance" Metrics 82

CHAPTER NINE: PROJECT ACCOUNTING 83
  Definition 83
  Project Finances – Background 84
  The Project Budget 84
  The Investment Appraisal Form 85
  The Project Budget Tracker 86

Project Accounting – Ongoing Tracking and Reporting 88
  PMO Analyst Role 88
    Purchase Orders 88
    Monthly Meetings 89

Regular Reviews 90
　PMO Manager's Role 90
　　Process Review 91
　　"At a Glance" Metrics 92

CHAPTER TEN: LESSONS LEARNED 93
　Definition 93
　The Participants 94
　The Process 94
　Identification 95
　The Lessons Learned Workshop 96
　　Sample Lessons Learned Questions 96
　　Five Whys Example 97
　The Lessons Learned Log 97
　Validation 98
　Action 98

Lessons Learned – Ongoing Management 99
　PMO Analyst Role 99
　PMO Manager Role 100

CHAPTER ELEVEN: DOCUMENT VERSION CONTROL 101
　Static Documents 101
　Version Control Tables 102
　Dynamic Documents 103

CHAPTER TWELVE: FINAL THOUGHTS 105
　What do I look for when recruiting PMO resources? 106
　Drive 106
　Passion 106
　Content Knowledge 107
　Loyalty 107

Foreword

When I started out in the world of IT I found myself in quite an unfamiliar place. I had just moved over from a career in retail management, and for once I wasn't quite sure where I was headed with the vast number of different opportunities on offer within IT. I knew with such a jump from retail to IT that I would have to start at the bottom and work my way up. However, the fast-paced world of IT offered lots of potential so it was a risk I was prepared to take. I had a couple of friends that were more established in IT, fulfilling PMO roles, and it all sounded quite exciting and varied, and it resonated with me as I've always been very organised and I like to think I can manage and motivate a team to get things done.

I started on a fixed-term contract as a project administrator on a Windows upgrade project from NT/4 to Windows XP SP2. It was a great starter project for me as upgrades aren't too dissimilar to the upgrades you perform on your home PCs, so I understood the scope and technicalities of the project from the outset. I've always been an extremely ambitious and driven individual, and this was something that I wanted to carry with me into my PMO career. Not only do I want to excel in my current role, but I also want to understand more about the role on the next step of the ladder. How does my manager complete their job? How would I do it differently? How would I work and push the boundaries of the role? I needed to establish a clear roadmap of my new career and an understanding of the timescales involved for each step along the way in order for me to achieve my goals.

Following that initial assignment there was a steep learning curve; I wanted to fully understand every facet of the PMO: what worked well? What didn't work so well? How can we do things better? Every role I undertook I was thinking about what I needed to learn in order for me to end that assignment in a position where I could apply for a more senior role. I moved between a number of different FTSE100 companies and pushed myself along the PMO career path through to management, and I'm now proud to be a PMO director leading the governance, reporting and portfolio PMO teams on one of the largest global SAP implementations there has ever been.

The organisation and structure of the PMO has always played to my strengths. However, it hasn't always offered the clear and prosperous career path that exists today. The PMO world is still in its infancy but it's growing fast; even just looking back across the period of the last few years, you can see a much greater understanding from organisations about the value a well-managed PMO can provide. The career PMO professionals are becoming more and more common, and working in a PMO is now seen to be a skill set and career in its own right and not simply a junior to the project or programme management teams.

Throughout my IT career I have been a consultant, so there is always an expectation when taking up a new assignment that I should be fully trained and hit the ground running. I believe that consultants should be the best in their field; they should be brought in by a company to make a real difference and lead the way on how that particular role should be fulfilled. This involves a lot of thought, research and training into each of my future roles to ensure their remits are fully understood and I can implement best practice at all levels. Now, with the benefit of experience, this is easier to do; as an analyst or even a PMO manager, this was more difficult. I had gained some experience from previous clients, but how did I know if that was best practice? How did my abilities compare to other analysts or managers in the market?

By writing this book, I wanted to give you my take on the world of the PMO. PMO functions and their objectives differ vastly from organisation to organisation; however, the basic controls and how these are executed should be very similar and share the same best practices.

The majority of textbooks focus on how to establish a PMO, understanding the stakeholders' requirements and how to ensure the PMO aligns strategically with the organisation. The aim for me was to start from the bottom up. What does best practice look like across the PMO controls, and what contributions should the PMO analysts and managers be making in order to demonstrate a best-in-class PMO. If you are considering a move to the world of PMO or you are an already established PMO professional, you can understand where your knowledge levels are, how to become the best you can be in your current role and also demonstrate what is required to reach the next level on the PMO career path.

Mark Readman

Connect with me on Twitter: @MR_PMO

Chapter One
The Beginning – What is a PMO?

The term PMO means many different things to many different people. This is largely due to the PMO being a relatively new function, but also one that has gathered a lot of momentum and come to people's attention over the last ten years.

> A PMO is a group or department within an organisation that defines and maintains standards for project management within the project or programme of work.

The PMO aims to align ways of working, processes and tools across the projects under its control. This will often involve initially defining these standards and then ensuring future projects adhere to them, or it may be reaching out to the wider organisation to understand the enterprise standards that are in place that should be used across all projects.

Reality vs Textbook

The most common use of the term PMO is "Programme Management Office", however, this isn't applied consistently. PMO is also used to describe a project office, portfolio management office or many more things relating to project management. Broadly, a PMO will be aligned to a project, a programme or a portfolio and will govern the project management practices and standards for all of the projects within their remit.

Unless the PMOs within a particular company were defined, structured, communicated and executed by one of the big consulting companies, the PMO was probably set up by a number of different individual consultants; one that has changed many times depending on the different sponsors' individual requirements or by the next consultant to take over the management of the PMO. This uncertainty and constant change leads to the ambiguity around what a PMO is all about and is the reason most PMOs differ from the number of textbook definitions you will have read about.

The PMO Resources

Keeping in the spirit of the often misunderstood meaning of the term PMO, the roles within the PMO also differ from organisation to organisation. However, there are usually three levels, the PMO analyst, the PMO manager and, in larger organisations, a PMO director or head of PMO.

The PMO Analyst

The PMO analyst can also be called a project or programme analyst, project\programme or PMO coordinator or even sometimes a project\programme or PMO administrator, although this is not as common as there tends to be dedicated admin resources allocated to this role.

If the PMO analyst is aligned to a project, they will be the gatherers of information and often the project manager's right-hand person. They will understand the detail of the project and the content of all of the project's outputs and controls.

If they are aligned to a programme, the analyst will work closely with the programme manager; depending on the size of the programme the analyst may be a step removed from the detail but still have a good level of understanding. Collecting project level data, aggregating this up to a programme level and compiling reports are key to this role.

Process Expertise

The aim for the PMO analyst is to be **THE** point of contact for questions on the PMO controls and processes across the project or programme. The PMO analyst must know and understand these controls inside out and establish themselves as the "Go-To" person for guidance and process questions.

It's particularly important to understand the different forums and meetings throughout a process, alongside the inputs and outputs required for each of these. Project managers seeking process guidance will always want to know:

- What is the next step?
- What do I need to have completed before I go to the meeting?
- What templates need to be filled out?
- Who should I have spoken to?
- What is the purpose of the meeting?
- How does the meeting run? What questions will I be asked?
- What are the outputs from this meeting?
- What are the next steps?

Managing the Project Managers

The relationship between the PMO analyst and the project manager is very important. It's key that the PMO analyst demonstrates value to the project and is welcomed as part of the project team. When initially being assigned to a project, the PMO analyst should meet with the project manager to initially discuss the scope of the project and what the project is in place to deliver.

The meeting should then walk through the PMO controls one by one and ensure the correct meetings and reporting timelines are in place. The PMO analyst can then offer training sessions to the project manager and project team on any of the PMO controls that require strengthening or improving. Offering training workshops is a great way to add value to a project and also helps to get endorsement from the project team into a particular process.

The PMO Manager

The PMO manager (or PMO lead) role will be assigned to a specific programme of work and aligned to a programme manager. Depending on the size and complexity of the programme, this may mean one or a number of PMO analysts report to the PMO manager.

When reading through this book, it is assumed that the manager understands and has experience of the activities described in the analyst sections in addition to learning or completing the activities described in the manager sections. You have to have the base foundation knowledge of the PMO analyst to truly be an effective PMO manager.

Content Knowledge

Aside from providing the detailed process knowledge, the PMO manager should understand the content of each of the PMO inputs when working at programme level. Taking the inputs from the PMO analysts and working alongside the programme manager, it's important to ask questions that enable the understanding of a particular statement, risk or issue, as well as completing the checks to ensure they are being correctly managed.

Are all of the points written on a project's status report clearly understood? What is the reason that a particular risk is running overdue and tracking as red? What are the interactions the two projects need to make to effectively manage a particular dependency?

Data Collection and Metrics

When joining an already existing PMO for projects that are already in flight, there should be a good amount of data available across the PMO controls that can be utilised; this could be in the form of a project and portfolio management (PPM) tool, project risks logs, change control documentation, status reports etc.

It is always worth putting in the time to review this data and organise it with a view to creating some meaningful metrics. This will give you a great "As Is" view of the current status of the project or programme across the different PMO controls; these can then be reported each week to show trends, recurring issues or themes. Once this data is collected, it enables the tracking of progress and performance over a specific period of time: for example, three months ago project X had fifteen risks overdue, and this week project X has zero overdue.

> Whenever I start a new assignment I want to get hold of as much existing data as possible. It's important for me to understand the starting point across all of the PMO controls. This then helps me decide upon some next steps that add value quickly and also helps determine the long-term plan to build up the maturity levels of the PMO.

Root Cause Mindset
If the PMO manager is very familiar with a particular programme of work, they can review the current and historic risk, issue and dependency data and understand the recurring themes, apply some root cause analysis techniques and work out the tangible actions for the project teams or workstream leads. Why is this risk raised project after project? What is preventing the root cause from being addressed?

Establishing a root cause mindset on all projects or programmes will pay dividends for future projects. If the team can mitigate the risk and at the same time address the root cause ensuring the risk doesn't reoccur, then future projects have a greater chance of success.

Add Value Quickly
There are three simple ways to add value very quickly when starting a new PMO role, and these can be applied across all of the PMO controls.

1. Process review (and where possible simplification).
2. Create valuable "At a Glance" metrics.
3. Address the root causes.

Following on from being **THE** point of contact and the process champion, it's important for the PMO manager to be noted for their emails and communication. Project and programme delivery is always a busy function and can also be very intense. If their communications are clear, show "At a Glance" metrics, defined actions or demonstrate simple process improvements, the PMO manager will quickly be seen as an individual that makes a real difference. Project and programme managers receive hundreds of emails every day. It's important that the interactions are clear and give the right answer every time.

The Head of PMO\PMO Director

PMO directors usually only exist in larger organisations with enterprise PMOs that justify this role as head of function. If the programme is of a large enough scale, it may have a PMO director leading the PMO for the programme. However, it is more common for the PMO director to be responsible for PMO activities at a portfolio level or even for the IT or organisation-wide PMO activities, with a team of managers and analysts reporting to them.

If you have worked your way through the analyst and management ranks and understand the level of detail described in each PMO control throughout this book, you should already be a PMO "heavy hitter" that can create PMOs from a blank canvas, or you can troubleshoot and optimise any area of existing PMOs.

The PMO director will take a more strategic view of the PMO and look across the whole portfolio of projects within their remit:

- How can the PMO(s) contribute to the mission and goals of the business?
- What types of PMO do we have? What types of PMO do we want to have?
- How can the PMO(s) better support the projects and programmes?
- How can we increase the maturity of the PMO(s)?
- How can we further establish the PMO(s) as a centre of excellence?

Each of these are lengthy topics in their own right, and therefore further research and a full understanding of these are a must for any aspiring PMO director.

Chapter Two
Meeting Support and Facilitation

One of the important tasks for PMO resources is to provide meeting facilitation and administrative support at the various meetings and workshops that they attend as part of their role.

It may seem strange to have a chapter on something that on the surface is quite basic, but effectively planning and managing meetings is a skill in itself. Projects are pressurised environments and people's time is in high demand. Therefore it's imperative to maximise the effectiveness of every meeting and ensure they achieve their objectives.

Meeting Invites

Meeting invites in an ideal world should be sent out well in advance of the meeting. The invites should include a clear meeting title and the time and location for the meeting along with a structured agenda. The body of the invite should always describe the meeting purpose and detail any requirements or expectations of the meeting attendees. Any documentation that is required to be reviewed by the meeting participants prior to the meeting should be attached.

> Familiarise yourself with the room booking process and any associated systems. The last thing you want to happen when all of the participants arrive at the meeting room is for there to be a problem with the booking and you are left without a meeting room!

```
                                              AGENDA
   PMO Service Overview
   December 4, 2014
   13.30 – 16.30

   Meeting called by Mark Readman

   Attendees



   Agenda

      • Introductions – Mark Readman – 5 mins
      • PMO Overview – Mark Readman – 15 mins
      • Etc
      • Etc
```

Figure 1. Meeting agenda example.

Room Preparation

Where possible, rooms should be prepared fifteen minutes before the meeting so the laptop and the projector or screen can be set up. Also, if required, the telephone conference call can be opened for the participants that cannot attend the meeting in person.

Meeting Management

To ensure a meeting is as effective as possible it's good practice to distribute some roles and responsibilities amongst the meeting attendees. These would be:

Chairperson – The owner and leader of the meeting.

Timekeeper – To ensure the meeting stays on track and as per the timings on the agenda. It's important to ensure subtopics are not discussed in too much detail; if required a side meeting should be advised.

Note Taker – To capture the minutes and actions from the meeting.

Minutes and Actions

The term "minutes" actually refers to the logging of decisions that are made, the planned next steps and who is going to complete these tasks. Taking minutes is not the task of noting down an exact transcript of the meeting discussions.
The benefits of logging minutes and actions are:

- To provide an accurate written record of the meeting, documenting what has been decided and who is going to action the next steps.
- Team members that were unable to attend the meeting can be kept informed.
- New team members can catch up on progress by reading previous meeting minutes.

When logging actions, a clear record should be kept of the agreed due date. This way the PMO can challenge this at each meeting and hold team members to account when the actions become overdue.

Meeting Tips

Initially when a PMO resource joins the project, they probably won't fully understand all of the content of the meetings, but there are some tips and best practices that can be used to ensure the minutes and actions are all captured accurately.

Table 1. Meeting Tips

Problem	Solution
Problems are being discussed but the resolution isn't clear.	Ask the group – "Is there an action required here?"
An action is being discussed but some of the decisions or action content has been missed.	Ask the group – "Can I just clarify the action there?" Then read the statement back to the group.
The discussion is difficult to follow because a number of people are talking at once and switching between agenda items.	It is reasonable to ask the group to speak one at a time and ask for clarification on which agenda item they are discussing.
It's unclear what has been agreed as several different suggestions have been made.	Ask the chairperson to clarify the decision that has been made.
An important decision has been made and it needs to be recorded correctly.	Read back the proposal/decision to the group to ensure accuracy.

Chapter Three
Status Reporting

Definition

Effective communication is a key component of successful project management. A large proportion of a project manager's role involves clear communication with the team and the project's stakeholders. The chances of project success are significantly increased if any communication issues are addressed early and a best practice standard for project communications is put in place.

> Project status reporting is the process of providing a regular, standardised evaluation of the project's progress against the plan. Its purpose is to effectively and efficiently communicate project status at regular intervals to project stakeholders.

Project status reporting is one of the most important methods of project communication. Project status reporting keeps the project team and stakeholders informed of the health of the project using a number of indicators like schedule, risks, issues, budget and scope. Keeping the project and stakeholder community informed enables the management to take action and key decisions (hopefully!) ahead of issues becoming critical.

Project status reports are a good way to document the history of a project. These can then be used to educate new project team members on the journey and the current status. These can also be a reminder to the project team when reviewing the content in preparation for a lessons learned workshop.

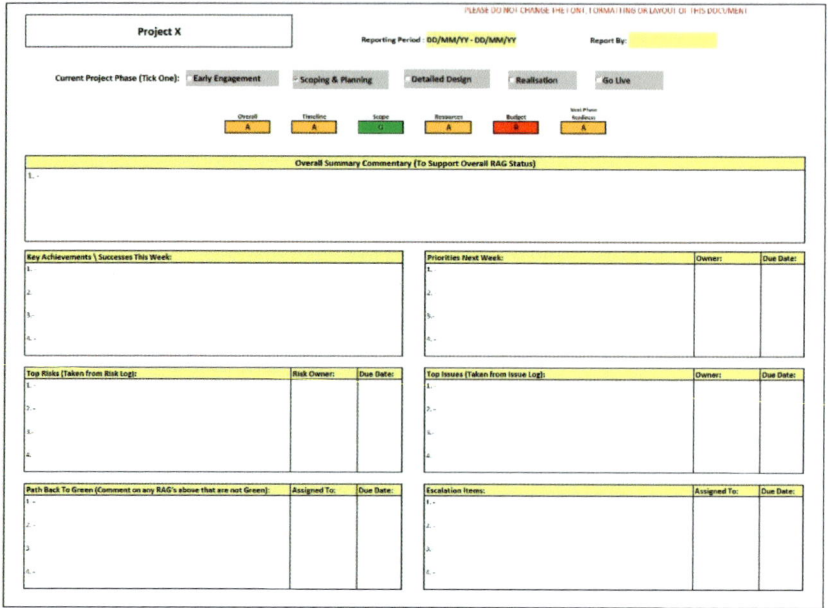

Figure 2. An example of a project status report.

The Reporting Cycle

Projects should report their status weekly, and these reports should be distributed on the same day each week to get the project team and stakeholders used to the reporting cycle. Reporting requirements do vary from project to project due to the size of an organisation, the level of information required, the type of project that is being completed and the level of complexity or risk.

Additional information or project reporting requirements should be identified early on in the project. This can evolve as the project progresses but should be defined early. Projects are likely to report additional information more frequently during key stages in the lifecycle; for example, through testing.

Depending on the set-up of the projects within the organisation, the project manager would normally provide the project status report to the PMO weekly, for inclusion in a wider programme reporting pack.

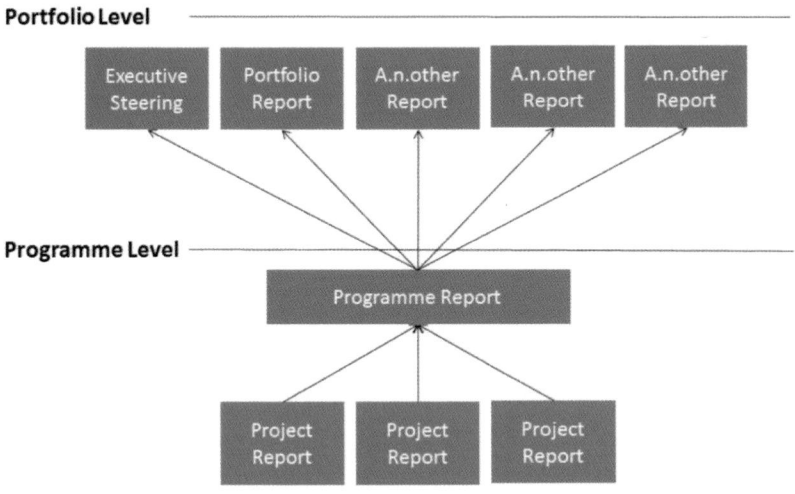

Figure 3. The project reporting flow.

The project manager may also distribute the status report to the project team and stakeholders separately, if required, or as defined in the project communications plan. It is important to note that formal status reporting is not a substitution for ongoing project communication between the project manager, project team, stakeholders, senior management, and any other parties needing updated project information.

Reporting – Ongoing Management

Meetings and Regular Reviews

The project status report will often be reviewed as part of the project team meeting. This gives a framework and structure to the meeting to ensure all critical areas of the project are reviewed and discussed. The project team meetings should be scheduled with the reporting cycle in mind to ensure that the most up-to-date project information is available for review at the meeting.

PMO Analyst Role

It is each of the project managers' responsibility to complete a status report when required. The PMO should define the reporting frequency and the report format along with any guidance required on how to populate the report.

When the status reports are received, the PMO analyst should check the content to ensure they fully understand it, but also to ensure the right level of information has been reported.

PMO Manager's Role

Process Review

Usually, the portfolio-wide reporting cycle will already be in place and it will be the PMO's role to ensure that the projects and programmes under their control report correctly to these timescales. If the reporting timelines are yet to be defined, then it tends to work best when requesting that the project status reports be submitted by the close of business each Thursday, or by midday each Friday. That way the reports can be collated by the PMO early on Friday afternoon and distributed, enabling the project teams and senior management to have up-to-date information on all of the projects by Monday morning each week.

Table 2. Status Report Review

Field	PMO Review Criteria
Overall Project Summary	This should contain a non-technical overview of where the project is this week against the schedule and the activities that were completed in the previous week. This should support the overall red, amber, green (RAG) status that has been selected.
Top Risks	These should match the entries in the risk log and have been written in the correct format: <Cause><Event><Effect> * More detail is provided in the Risk and Issue Management chapter.
Top Issues	These should match the entries in the issue log and have been written in the correct format: <Cause><Event><Effect> * More detail is provided in the Risk and Issue Management chapter.
Path Back to Green	Any of the RAG statuses that have been selected as amber or red should be explained here. This is good as it encourages the project manager to think about remediation plans.
Escalation Items	This should contain details of any help required by the senior management or the project sponsor.

Programme Level Reporting

The PMO manager will collate the project status reports into a programme level reports pack. This should be the programme manager's bible that each week shows the exact status of all of the projects, the top risks and issues across the programme, any dependencies and where the projects are against their plans.

The programme reports pack contents will be defined by the programme manager. Some of the more common inputs that could be included are:

- Programme roadmap – An overview by phase (Chevron diagram or Gantt chart) of all of the projects within the programme.
- Risk and issue management summary – An "At a Glance" view of the top programme and project risks and issues.
- Plan summary report – An overview of each of the projects' current progress against the original plan, alongside a report detailing any overdue milestones or deliverables.
- Financial summary report – A summary of the programme's financial position against the allocated budget and the latest forecast.
- Each of the project status reports for the projects within the programme.

Chapter Four
Project Schedule

Definition

Project planning is the method of defining how a project will be completed within a certain timeframe, utilising a predefined methodology and project stages with allocated resources.

Project Schedule vs Project Plan

The project schedule is a timeline of a project's activities, deliverables, milestones, resources and dependencies. The schedule depicts what is to be completed, by whom and by when. This is most commonly reflected in a list of tasks and a Gantt chart. A Microsoft Project document is a project schedule.

A project plan is a set of documents designed to guide the control and execution of a project. This will include the project schedule, but also:

- Assumptions\decisions
- Risks
- Issues
- Deliverables
- Resources
- Costs
- Checkpoints and phase exits

- External dependencies

An effective plan is one which brings each of these components together, allowing views of the plan to be taken that meet the needs of varying audiences but originate from the same source of data.

A project plan is key to a successful project and is the most important document set that needs to be created and maintained throughout the project.

Reality vs Textbook

It's fair to say that the definitions of a project plan and a project schedule are largely misunderstood. Ninety-five per cent of the companies that I have worked with talk about their Microsoft Project plan document when referring to their project plan. This, of course, is in fact their project schedule!

As the other controls within the project plan, apart from the project schedule, are covered in different sections within this book, we will concentrate for the remainder of this chapter on the project schedule.

The Levels of Project Schedule

Typically, there are three levels when scheduling a project:

- The level 1 (low detail) schedule is the "Plan on a Page". This depicts the project phases, major deliverables and milestones. This is often in a Microsoft PowerPoint or Excel format and is used to give a high-level view of the project's lifecycle.

- Level 2 (medium detail) schedules are at the next level of detail, combining elements of project methodology, key activities, deliverables, task ownership and milestones.

- The level 3 (high detail) schedules are at the very detailed level. Inputs to level 3 schedules should be detailed workstream plans including the detail from specific trackers where applicable. These can then be summarised in an overall project level 3 schedule.

In some cases, the project manager may decide to combine the level 2 and 3 schedules as their preferred way to track the project. In this case, it is best practice to expect the schedule to be detailed to level 3 for the next three months, then detailed to level 2 after that until the end of the project.

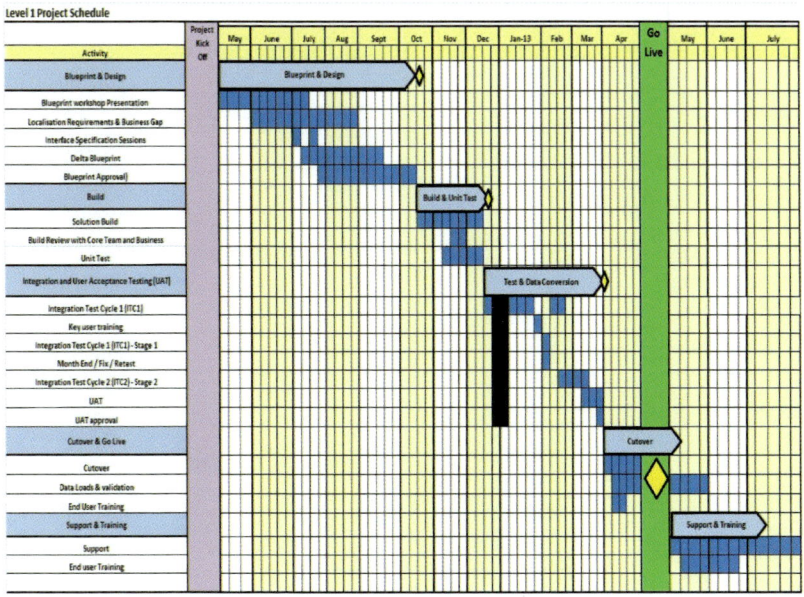

Figure 4. Level 1 project schedule example.

Resource Management

In project terms, resources are the human or capital requirements needed to complete the tasks on the project schedule. Human resources are the project team, stakeholders, customers or project suppliers. Capital resources are hardware, software or any other equipment or infrastructure required by the project.

A truly effective project schedule is one that has been resource loaded and levelled, giving the project manager a clear view of the resource constraints and requirements for the next phase of the project. The project manager should assign resources to the tasks on the level 3 schedule. Where possible this should be named resources. However, just adding the role required is sufficient until an actual person has been identified for the role.

Once these resource requirements have been captured, the project manager will need to formally request the resources needed for the project so they can be reserved to carry out the specified activities on the project. Each organisation will have a different way of requesting resources. In an ideal world this would all be completed through MS Project and the resource pool in MS Project Server, however, I'm yet to find a company that has this process down to a fine art!

PMO Analyst Role

Delivery against the project schedule is always the accountability of the project manager. They have the knowledge and experience on how to deliver the project. The project manager is therefore responsible for producing the project schedule by taking inputs from the project team and workstream leads. This is the case for all but the largest projects. These projects may have a dedicated project planner assigned to provide specialist scheduling knowledge and take the responsibility of updating and maintaining the schedules away from the project manager.

For the majority of PMO analysts, the role of scheduling is out of their scope, however, they can often be asked to provide administrative support to the project manager when completing their schedules or collating the workstream leads updates.

> The tool of choice for level 2 and 3 project scheduling is Microsoft Project. It's worth investing in some training on the basics through to advanced knowledge of Microsoft Project to give an overview of the features and reports that can be generated.
>
> A valuable activity would be to volunteer to work alongside the project manager on the schedule updates. You can then fully understand all of the steps in the schedule through to delivery. You will work closer with the workstream leads on their updates and understand the impacts of their information on the overall schedule.

PMO analysts should familiarise themselves with the resource management processes within the organisation so they can support the project managers when submitting their resource plans and when securing the required resources for the project. Effective resource management is a key success factor for any project, and submitting the resource plans as early as possible so the required resources can be allocated to the project only increases the chance of success.

Project Schedule Assurance

With the activity of project scheduling being largely outside of the PMO analysts role, it's still important to have a good understanding of "best practice" and also any related timelines within the organisation (schedules to be updated weekly, or on a particular day each week).

If required to do so by the PMO manager, the PMO analyst will need to complete quality reviews or assurance checks of the project schedules within the PMO. These cannot largely address any issues with the content, but can check to ensure the schedules are being created and managed in line with company or best practice.

Some examples of these quality checks are:

- Does the organisation have a standard project schedule template? If so, is it in use by the project?
- Does the schedule contain all of the major phases for delivery?
- Is the schedule completed at a detailed task level for the next three months, with a medium level of detail after that?
- Are there tasks with estimated durations in the detailed level part of the plan? If so, these tasks should be clarified with the relevant team member.
- Are there any tasks over twenty days in duration? If so, these tasks should be broken down into a lower level of detail.
- Has the critical path been highlighted?

- Has the schedule been baselined? Can variances to the baseline be measured?
- Has the schedule been resource loaded?

- Is the schedule showing any target dates in the past?
- Are the task relationships (predecessors\successors) being used?
- Tasks with fixed (hard constrained) dates should be kept to a minimum.

Chapter Five
Programme Schedule

Definition

A programme schedule is the integration of all of the project schedules within the programme into a single schedule. Always check with the programme manager to understand their requirements for an integrated programme schedule. This will then drive the level of detail needed to be pulled through from the individual project schedules.

For a programme schedule to be effective, integrating schedules at the most detailed level isn't usually required; an integrated level 2 plan should satisfy the requirement. Programme managers require visibility of items like project dependencies, when a particular project is passing through the different environments or key milestones. Task level detail is managed by the project manager and reviewed by the programme manager by exception.

PMO Manager's Role

The PMO manager will be very familiar with the project lifecycle and the standard activities that are required through each phase of the project. The PMO manager's content knowledge should be significantly higher than the PMO analyst; they will have completed a number of end-to-end project deployments previously and also be well versed in the use of planning tools like Microsoft Excel and Microsoft Project, at least to an administration level.

Process Review

The PMO manager will need to fully understand the project planning cycle. If there is a particular time in the week that the programme schedules are collated from the project schedule information, then it's imperative that the project schedules are fully up to date by that point in the week.

In the absence of a specific project planning team, it may become the task of the PMO manager to integrate all of the level 2 project schedules for the programme into an integrated programme schedule. Therefore the PMO manager can define or influence the project planning cycle.

It's important to plug into the programme dependency management process so that the dependent tasks can be linked at programme level and possible implications can be assessed as early as possible.

"At a Glance" Metrics

The plans should be set up to facilitate the creation of reports and metrics. These can then be reviewed with the programme manager and actioned accordingly. The schedule is one of the most important project documents and is used to understand if the project is on track or not. The PMO manager should carefully monitor and question the plan versions that are submitted weekly for integration into the programme plan.

When receiving a plan update, the following points should be reviewed and questioned:

- Have any of the milestone dates been moved?

- Has the "Go Live" date been affected by the recent plan changes?
- Have the project phase completion dates been changed?
- How does this plan update affect the programme level dependent tasks?

These project and programme schedule reviews give early visibility of plan changes and should be used to aid discussions about the impact of these plan changes or used as a trigger to review the plan in detail to understand how the project or programme can be brought back on schedule.

Chapter Six
Risk and Issue Management

Risks

The environment of project delivery is ever changing and quite unpredictable. Projects rarely run according to plan. The process of risk management gives each project a mechanism for handling this level of uncertainty. Project risk management is the identification, assessment and prioritisation of risks followed by a structured regular review. This, along with active management to control and mitigate the risks, should reduce the probability of risks becoming project issues. Project risk can be anything that threatens or limits the goals, objectives or deliverables of a project. It is far easier and less costly to avoid a risk, or reduce its impact, than it is to manage it if it occurs unexpectedly.

Definition

What is a risk in project terms? There are many definitions available explaining what a risk is. Personally, the easiest way I've found to think about it is: **a risk is something that might happen in the future and have an effect on the project or programme**.

> A risk is an uncertain event or set of events that, should they occur, will have a material effect on the achievement of the project's objectives (time, quality, cost, scope, benefits).

The Risk Log (Register)

The risk log is the central repository for storing details of all of the risks raised on the project. The fields required or used in a risk log tend to differ slightly from company to company, but there are a number of core fields that must be included for effective risk management.

Additional fields are often added to suit the level of governance required for risk management within the organisation, add further clarity to the risk or increase the maturity of the risk management metrics that can be generated.

Table 3. Core Field Examples

Field	Definition
Risk ID (Ref Number)	The unique identification number for the risk.
Level	Is this a risk to the project or the programme?
Date Raised	The date the risk was raised.
Originator (Raised by:)	The name of the individual who raised the risk.
Owner	The name of the individual who will own the risk.
Title	A short title for the risk.
Description	A description of the risk structured by cause, event and effect.
Status	This field can be amended to support the risk management reporting requirements. Some options are: Open, Deferred, Rejected, Approved, Overdue or Closed.
Impact	The impact value based on impact vs probability matrix.

Probability	The probability value based on impact vs probability matrix.
Risk Score	The RAG status – red, amber, green. The calculated impact vs probability value.
Mitigation Plan	The mitigation action plan demonstrating clear ownership and target dates.
Progress Updates	An update explaining the progress that has been made during this reporting period against the mitigation plan.
Due Date	The date the mitigating action is due.
Impact Date	The date when the risk will start to impact the project?
Commentary (Working Notes)	Progress commentary against the mitigation plan.
Closure Date	The date the risk is closed.

Table 4. Optional Field Examples

Field	Definition
Project	The Project name – used in a programme level risk log.
Impact Description	A description of the impacts of the risk? This can be separated if there is not enough detail is shown in the description field.
Impact Type	Impact type examples – Budget, Schedule, Quality, Resources, Architecture, Business Change, Scope, Other.
Escalation	The type of escalatory action is required. Action, information or intensive care.

Current Impact	The current impact level. To enable tracking against the original impact value, a current impact value is logged.
Current Probability	The current probability level. To enable tracking against the original probability value, a current probability value is logged.
Current Risk Score	The current RAG status – red, amber, green. The calculated impact vs probability value.
Next Review Date	The date the risk will next be reviewed.
Target Completion Date	The target date in which the risk will be mitigated.

Identification

Risk identification can take a number of forms depending on the size of the organisation and the size of the project and project team. These can range from brainstorming workshops and stakeholder interviews, through to email questionnaires and informal discussions.

The most effective strategy I've found when supporting project risk identification that can be applied to projects of most complexities and size is the following four-step approach, assuming, in advance, that the project stakeholders and the members of the project team have been identified and confirmed.

It's also worth noting that the following process should also lead to issues and dependencies being identified and captured.

1. A well-constructed email to the project stakeholders and project team explaining the definition of a risk and the purpose of this risk identification exercise. Depending on the complexity of the risk log, a blank version or cut-down version can be attached with some field definitions requesting the recipients add their thoughts on potential risks to the successful delivery of the project. It's important to ensure that a clear target date for completion of this identification exercise is communicated.

2. Plan to catch up with the project stakeholders and project team informally to talk through this request and ensure they are aware of the deadline. This is a good way of facilitating the discussion of potential risks that need to be raised and gives a greater understanding from the start of the risks facing the project.

3. The responses should be collated into a central risk log. Where the entries are clear, duplicates should be removed and any entries that require clarification or have been submitted with fields missing or incomplete should be marked for further review.

4. Hold a risk review workshop with the project team. The format of this workshop may differ on larger projects; there may be a requirement to divide the meeting into timeslots where the team is split into groups and attend at different stages throughout the meeting. The purpose of the meeting is to review all entries submitted to the risk log, ensure the risk is fully understood and to identify the risk owner. It's also important to highlight the due date for each risk along with the impact and probability rating so the entries can be categorised and managed accordingly. A takeaway action

from this meeting should be for the risk owners to complete the mitigation plan for their assigned risks before the next risk review meeting.

Following this process will provide a good starting position and indicates the initial level of risk facing the project or programme. It is important at this initial risk review meeting to communicate to the project team the ways in which the risks that are discovered in the future can be raised. In addition, the aim is to create a culture where concerns are openly discussed and there is a process in place to facilitate the assessment of these concerns, and formal risk management is applied where appropriate. The regular review process can now begin to track the progress and mitigation of the risks that have been discovered.

Description

An important aspect of risk identification is providing a clear and unambiguous expression of the risk. A risk should be described showing a clear cause, event and effect. For example:

> "Due to < **Cause**>, there is the risk of <**Event**> that could result in <**Effect**>."

<**Cause**> Describe the source of the risk, i.e. the situation that has given rise to the risk.
Handling a risk by addressing root causes is ultimately more effective than merely addressing symptoms or direct causes of risk.

<Event> Describe the area of risk in terms of threat, opportunity or uncertainty.

<Effect> Describe the impact(s) that the risk would have on the project\programme's objectives, should the risk materialise.

Risk Rating – Impact vs Probability Matrix

Risks need to be prioritised and scored so that they can be treated and reviewed accordingly. The most widely used scoring mechanism that drives the red, amber, green status of a risk is the impact vs probability matrix.

Table 5. Probability Value Examples

Level	Description	Probability
1	Very Low	0–5% likely to happen
2	Low	6–20% likely to happen
3	Medium	21–50% likely to happen
4	High	51–80% likely to happen
5	Very High	>80% likely to happen

Table 6. Impact Value Examples

Level	Description	Probability
1	Very Low	No measurable impact.
2	Low	Unlikely to have a significant effect on the project outcome.
3	Medium	Likely to have a significant impact but can be managed without major effect in the medium term.
4	High	Likely to have a significant effect that will require major effort and/or escalation to manage and resolve in the medium term and threatens the eventual project outcome.
5	Very High	If not resolved will severely effect project outcome.

Table 7. Impact vs Probability RAG Values

Green = 1–4

Amber = 5–11

Red = 12+

Probability	Impact				
	Very Low 1	Low 2	Medium 3	High 4	Very High 5
Very High 5	5	10	15	20	25
High 4	4	8	12	16	20
Medium 3	3	6	9	12	15
Low 2	2	4	6	8	10
Very Low 1	1	2	3	4	5

Mitigation Planning

It is the risk owner's responsibility to devise a mitigation plan that will reduce the likelihood of the risk occurring and/or reduce the impact of the risk.

A clear and well-defined mitigation plan is key to effective risk management. This plan should be agreed with all parties, showing a clear date of entry, clear ownership and a clear target completion date.

Mitigation plans should be a summary level step-by-step plan documenting how that particular risk will be mitigated. This

step-by-step plan should always drive the due date entry that is captured in the risk log.

> "Step 1. DD/MM/YY – <Mitigating Action><Name><Target Completion Date DD/MM/YY>"

> "Step 2. DD/MM/YY – <Mitigating Action><Name><Target Completion Date DD/MM/YY>"

> "Step 3. DD/MM/YY – <Mitigating Action><Name><Target Completion Date DD/MM/YY>"

As the mitigation plan is executed, the risk level should be regularly reviewed and revised accordingly. The revised risk scores can be recorded separately from the original ones. This is particularly useful for risk management reporting and valuable trend reporting.

Issues

Project issue management goes hand in hand with risk management and should be subject to the same level of governance as the management of risk. In many ways, an issue is more important as **an issue is something that is affecting the project right now and needs to be actively managed.**

It is the responsibility of the project manager to effectively manage and monitor issues on a regular basis and follow up with the issue owners to ensure progress is being made towards the resolution.

Definition

Project issues must be identified, controlled and managed throughout the lifecycle of the project in order for the project to be successful. Issue management addresses obstacles that have an effect on one of more of the project's objectives. The purpose of issue management is to identify and document these issues and manage them through to closure in a controlled environment, allowing the review of all relevant information.

> A project issue is an event that has occurred and either has a positive or negative effect on a project's chances of achieving its objectives.

The Issue Log (Register)

The issue log will usually be combined in the same workbook as the risk log (unless, of course, a PPM tool is in use to manage the issues). This is, in fact, best practice, as risks that become issues can easily be transferred and all risk and issue data is stored centrally in one location.

Like the risk log, there are a number of core fields required, along with some additional fields that can facilitate the production of more mature metrics or can be used to target specific areas of issue management that require more detailed attention.

Table 8. Core Field Examples

Field	Definition
Issue ID	The unique identification number for the issue.
Originator (Raised by:)	The name of the individual who raised the issue.
Owner	The name of the individual who will own the issue.
Title	A short title for the issue.
Description	A description of the issue. This should also include a description of the impact.
Date Raised	The date the issue was opened.
Due Date	The date the mitigating action is due.
Priority\Issue Score	The RAG status – red, amber, green. High, medium or low.
Issue Type	The type of issue. Budget, Schedule, Quality, Resources, Architecture, Bus. Change, Scope, Other.
Mitigation Plan	The mitigation action plan demonstrating clear ownership and target dates.
Status	This field can be amended to support the issue management reporting requirements. Some options are: Open, In Progress, Overdue or Closed.
Progress Updates	An update explaining the progress that has been made during this reporting period against the mitigation plan.

Escalation	The type of escalatory action required. Action, information or intensive care.
Closure Date	The date the issue was closed.
Commentary (Working Notes)	Progress commentary against the mitigation plan.

Table 9. Optional Field Examples

Field	Description
Project	The project name – Used in a programme level issue log.
Risk Reference	The original risk reference if a risk has been transferred to an issue.
Impact Description	A description of the impacts of the issue. These can be separated if there is not enough detail shown in the description field.
Next Review Date	The date the issue will next be reviewed.
Target Completion Date	The target date on which the issue will be fully mitigated.

Identification

By following the risk identification process described earlier, this will normally also lead to the identification of project and programme issues. These can then be categorised and logged correctly after the identification meeting.

If the project is in its early stages or at project kick-off, there will probably only be a handful of issues identified. However, it's important to capture these and put in place the plans for active management along with highlighting the avenues for the ongoing identification of issues.

The weekly project status meeting is the most common place for the identification of issues, so it's important to ensure there are methods in place to capture these. An important mindset for the PMO resources to establish when attending the weekly status meetings is to question – "Do we have an issue raised for this?" This then drives the right behaviour in highlighting the importance of capturing these issues and gets the whole project team thinking in the same way.

Description

Similar to the guidelines provided when describing a risk, it's equally important to clearly articulate the issues that are raised on the project or programme. This way, it is clear to the whole of the project team what the issue actually is that is affecting the project. Subsets of the issue log will always be used for management reporting, and if issues are described correctly from the outset, it saves a lot of rework later on.

An issue should be described showing a clear root cause, event and effect for example:

"Due to **< Cause>**, the following **<Event>** has occurred that has resulted in **<Effect>**."

<Cause> Describe the source of the issue, i.e. the situation that led to the issue arising.

<Event> Describe the area of uncertainty in terms of threat, opportunity or uncertainty.

<Effect> Describe the impact(s) that the issue may have on the programme's objectives. Issues should be specific, with impacts and actions quantified.

Issue Rating - Priority

Issues, by their nature, are events that are already affecting the project, therefore, unlike risks, there is no need to assign a probability rating. Issues are rated using a high, medium or low scoring that is aligned to a red (high), amber (medium) or green (low) colour rating (RAG) for reporting.

Red, amber, green (RAG) definitions will differ from organisation to organisation. Here's an example:

- High (red) – An issue that will have a high impact on the project's outcomes in terms of time, cost or quality or has the potential to stop the project completely.
- Medium (amber) – An issue that will have a noticeable impact on the project's time, cost or quality, but won't stop the project from proceeding.
- Low (green) – An issue that doesn't affect activities on the critical path, and has little impact on a project's time, cost or quality.

Depending on the size of the project and the level of governance required for issue management, a five-point priority scale may facilitate more in-depth tracking and reporting.

Very High = Red
High = Amber Red
Medium = Amber

Low = Amber Green
Very Low = Green

Mitigation Planning

It is the issue owner's responsibility to devise a mitigation plan for the issue. The principles for mitigation planning that were defined for risk management should also be followed for issue management. The plan should be agreed with all parties, showing a clear date of entry, clear ownership and a clear target completion date.

> "Step 1. DD/MM/YY – <Mitigating Action><Name><Target Completion Date DD/MM/YY>"
> "Step 2. DD/MM/YY – <Mitigating Action><Name><Target Completion Date DD/MM/YY>"
> "Step 3. DD/MM/YY – <Mitigating Action><Name><Target Completion Date DD/MM/YY>"

Mitigation plans should always drive the due date entry that is captured in the issue log.

Risks and Issues – Ongoing Management

Progress Updates

Progress updates should clearly show progress since the last review against the item's mitigation plan. Updates should be concise and understandable by any audience (i.e. non-technical). Good practice would be to prefix each update with the initials of the person providing the update, along with the date the update was provided. For example – MR070814.

Meetings and Regular Reviews

Following the initial risk and issue identification meeting, there is a need to define the frequency and format of ongoing reviews. The frequency and format differs depending on the project size and the level of governance in place for risk and issue management across the organisation.

The best practice standard is that all risks and issues in the log are reviewed and updated once per week. Risks or issues that are categorised as high or greater should be updated more frequently, in some cases daily.

The most common form of review is a weekly meeting with the PMO analyst and the project manager combined with a weekly risk and issue review board meeting. This is usually chaired by the programme manager, in which "High" entries and all programme risks and issues are reviewed.

The PMO analyst and project manager review ensures the risks and issues are updated and are being actively managed. It also gives the opportunity for the PMO analyst to quality check against the process documentation and ensures the log is being completed correctly and in line with best practice.

A weekly programme risk and issue review board provides the opportunity for "High" and programme entries to be reviewed by the programme leadership team and escalated accordingly. It is also an important time for the programme management to reinforce best practice risk and issue management and ensure the project is complying with the process.

PMO Analyst Role

Risk and issue management are two key PMO controls. If the processes are well-defined and efficient, there is lots of value that can be delivered as a result. If they are not working so well, the processes will often not be followed and reporting risks and issues will be seen as a burden or admin task.

The analyst should complete weekly or fortnightly reviews with the project managers. These meetings ensure that the risks and issues on a project are being managed correctly and are compliant with the process. This precious review time with the project manager should also be utilised to fully understand the content of the risks and issues currently being faced by the project. In larger projects this may not be possible, but the content of the high risks and issues should be understood.

Key things to look out for when completing reviews and quality checks:

- Has the risk\issue been written correctly? <Cause><Event><Effect>
- Has the owner been agreed?
- Does the mitigation plan show clear ownership and target dates?
- Does the target date quoted in the mitigation plan match the due date field?
- Is the risk\issue overdue?
- Has the impact\probability rating or issue priority been assigned correctly?
- Does the risk\issue require escalation?
- Have the closed entries been closed correctly? Including an accurate closure statement?

The one-to-one meetings with the project manager are the perfect way to reinforce that risks and issues must be managed and compliant with the process. Risks and issues that are currently overdue either do not have a mitigation plan in place or the mitigation plan has broken down and this is not an acceptable place to be.

By having good attention to detail and expert process knowledge, the PMO analyst can quickly establish themself as someone that adds real value, provides an excellent depth of knowledge and an excellent service to the project management community.

PMO Manager's Role

Process Review

Similar to the analyst, a comprehensive review must start with the existing process and supporting documentation. Knowing the PMO processes inside out is a must for a PMO manager. The difference here is that the PMO manager should be able to demonstrate potential improvements to the process and also areas where the organisation is not aligned with best practice.

- Is the method for identifying risks\issues effective?
- Do risks\issues require approval? What is the approval process?
- When were the project team last trained on risk\issue management?
- How are the risk\issue reviews completed?
- What tool are we using to log risks\issues?
- How can the process be improved?
- What metrics\reports are currently being circulated?

Following this review, and depending on the level of competency across the project team for risk and issue management, it may be worth planning a refresher or relaunch across the project. This is a good way to baseline knowledge, demonstrate a new and improved process, and reset roles, responsibilities and expectations.

Once the process has been reshaped or relaunched, a plan can be established with the PMO analyst to regularly review the logs with the project manager. The checks carried out should include those listed earlier in the PMO analyst section. It's also worth reiterating the rules for the escalation of a risk to the risk management board. This could be high project risks, programme level risks and any other risks flagged as part of the PMO analyst review.

"At a Glance" Metrics

There is likely to be lots of historic data available on risks and issues across the projects, either in the form of Excel logs or within a project and portfolio management (PPM) Tool. The PMO manager should invest the time to trawl through this data, remodel it into a useable format and produce a set of "As Is" metrics, along with trends to communicate the current position on risk and issue management across the projects.

Keeping the metrics simple and "At a Glance" can be a powerful tool that can be positioned alongside the process refresh\relaunch to really get the organisation focussed on risk and issue management.

Some examples of these metrics are:

- The number of risks\issues opened each week.
- The number of risks\issues closed each week.
- The open vs closed numbers each week.
- Average open time of a risk\issue.
- The number of high risks\issues.
- The percentage of risks\issues that is high.
- The number of risks\issues without a mitigation plan.
- The number of overdue risks\issues.
- The number of times a risk\issue due date has changed.
- The risks\issues that are due in the next week\fortnight\thirty days.

Once these items are being tracked weekly, some powerful reports can be produced for the project and senior management to demonstrate the current performance levels on risk and issue management.

It is important for the PMO analyst and manager to know and understand the metrics on their projects and programme. This is a good way of challenging project managers when required, and working together to improve the position of the metrics.

An example of a question to ask on the red risks would be: "If this risk became an issue, what is the impact on the project plan or the critical path". The PMO analyst can then support the project manager in planning out that scenario to understand if it is recoverable or requires escalation.

Address the Root Causes

Aside from the metrics, it's important to understand the content of the entries raised on the projects or programmes. Once the PMO manager has gained that level of detailed knowledge, the risks or issues that appear again and again from project to project can be tracked, and root causes can be highlighted and addressed.

It could be a particular team that isn't managed effectively, a certain type of resource that is quite scarce, planning inaccuracies, scope creep or many more. However, tracing back the root cause and proposing a plan to address the issues is a PMO service that goes the extra mile and adds real value.

Chapter Seven
Dependency Management

Definition

The A dependency acknowledges the relationship between activities associated with a project or programme. One or more activities may be reliant on another in order to be started or completed successfully. There are two main types of dependencies:

> **Internal Dependencies**
> Activities that one project is reliant on happening before something else can happen, all within the scope of the same project. A simple example would be that testing cannot happen unless the software is actually designed and built.
> **External Dependencies**
> Activities outside of the scope of one project that need to happen before a certain activity on another project can take place.

The Dependency Log (Register)

Dependencies should always be thought about as a particular type of risk that needs to be managed. Therefore, it's good practice to add the dependency log to the same workbook alongside the risk and issue logs. That way dependencies can easily be transferred across to risks or issues should the need arise. This will work fine for internal dependencies. However, dependencies, in their nature, have a dependent group and an enabling team or project.

Therefore, external dependencies should be logged by the wider group to facilitate visibility and updates by all parties.

For example, an external dependency affecting a project would need to be logged in a programme level dependency log. An external dependency affecting a programme should be logged in a portfolio dependency log.

For ease, I have always split and colour-coded the log into two sections to record information for the dependent and enabling parties on the project.

Table 10. Core Field Examples

Field	Definition
Dependency ID (Ref Number)	The unique identification number for the dependency.
Level	Is this a dependency between projects or programmes?
Date Raised	The date the dependency was raised.
Description	A clear, non-technical description of the dependency.
Priority	The RAG status – red, amber, green. High, medium or low.
Next Review Date	The date the dependency will next be reviewed.
Dependent Section	
Programme	The name of the dependent programme.
Project	The name of the dependent project.
Workstream	The name of the dependent workstream.
Owner	The name of the individual from the dependent project who will own the dependency.

Impact Date	The date the dependency will start to impact the project if it is not mitigated.
Impact Description	A description of the impact and implications on the project.
Enabling Section	
Programme	The name of the enabling programme.
Project	The name of the enabling project.
Workstream	The name of the enabling workstream.
Owner	The name of the individual from the enabling project who will own the dependency.
Delivery Date	The date the dependency actions will be delivered.
Mitigation Plan	The mitigation action plan demonstrating clear ownership and target dates.

Identification

Dependency identification can be a little more in-depth than the identification of risks and issues, as there is the added complexity of trying to identify all external dependencies.

Starting with the risk and issue identification process described earlier will lead to the identification of many internal dependencies. It may also lead to the discovery of some external dependencies that then require further investigation.

Stakeholder interviews are a great way to get an insight into the wider organisation and can often lead to uncovering external dependencies. This will also give stakeholders more time to think about these than solely in the risk and issue identification sessions.

It's also worthwhile reviewing any roadmaps or integrated plans in place for the wider organisation as this will lead to other areas of investigation. In addition, if there are any reporting requirements to external departments or areas of the business, then some discussions with those recipients can also help build up a full picture of activities across the organisation, and that in turn helps with the discovery of external dependencies.

Description

Unlike risks and issues, there is no standard way for describing a dependency. However, the rule that should be applied is that the description should be clear, non-technical and easily understood if it was being read by someone external to the project. The description should include high-level details of the activities that need to happen, by whom and when they need to have been completed.

The impact description should follow the same rule and describe the implications on the project if the dependency was not addressed and managed to a resolution.

Dependency Rating – Priority

Priority ratings for dependencies are assigned in the same way as issues and are driven by the time remaining until reaching the impact date, although the timing tolerances will differ depending on the organisation.

Here are some example definitions:

- High (red) – Dependencies that require resolution within the next two weeks.
- Medium (amber) – Dependencies that require resolution within the next two to four weeks.
- Low (green) – Dependencies that require resolution within the next four to eight weeks, or longer.

Mitigation Planning

It is the dependency owner from the enabling project that has the responsibility to devise an acceptable mitigation plan for the dependency.

The plan should be agreed with all parties, showing a clear date of entry, clear ownership and a clear target completion date.

"Step 1. DD/MM/YY – <Mitigating Action><Name><Target Completion Date DD/MM/YY>"

"Step 2. DD/MM/YY – <Mitigating Action><Name><Target Completion Date DD/MM/YY>"

"Step 3. DD/MM/YY – <Mitigating Action><Name><Target Completion Date DD/MM/YY>"

Approved mitigation plans for dependencies should always have a completion date that is **before** the impact date.

Dependencies – Ongoing Management

Meetings and Regular Reviews

Due to the similarities in nature and process of dependencies and risks, the dependency reviews should take place alongside the regular reviews of risks and issues. As noted previously this may be one-to-one reviews with the PMO analyst, or dependencies may become an agenda item for the weekly risk and issue review board.

There is another aspect to dependency management and that is the discovery phase. It's important to always stay up to date with the wider changes and the roadmap that has been put in place by the organisation. The PMO manager should try to have a dependency discovery mindset. For example, if a new project is starting – what is the scope of the new project? What are the potential touch points between the new project and the projects or programme within their remit? If potential dependencies are highlighted, it's a good idea to attend the new project's risk identification session to formally log any dependencies. In addition, this builds up relationships and contacts with the new project manager and the project team.

PMO Analyst Role

Like all PMO processes, the PMO analyst should really strive to be the knowledge base of how the process is working at grass-roots level. How are dependencies managed within the project or programme? How are external programme dependencies tracked? It's worth getting to know this level of detail, understand the content, the next steps, who to contact, and the inputs and outputs for each of the forums or meetings throughout the process.

Dependency updates should be taken when meeting with the project managers to review their risks and issues. This will not only add a check step to ensure that the dependencies on a project are being managed correctly and are compliant with the process, but it will also provide valuable one-to-one time to fully understand the content of the dependency.

Key things to look out for when completing reviews and quality checks:

- Has the dependency been written correctly? Has non-technical language that clearly articulates the dependency been used?
- Has ownership been agreed on the dependent and enabling side?
- Does the mitigation plan show clear ownership and target dates?
- Does the mitigation plan show exactly the steps that need to happen by both the dependent and enabling parties in order to successfully mitigate the dependency?
- Are any of the dependency actions overdue?

PMO Manager's Role

Process Review

After undertaking the normal process review and validating all of the process steps with the PMO analyst, there should then be a period of review and feedback with the wider project community to highlight any potential improvements that can be made to the process. Process review and improvement is quite a laborious task and often undertaken far too infrequently. Teams normally put up with a slightly inefficient process in favour of completing a full review. However, as the PMO manager new to the role or organisation, this is a step that is well worth undertaking. The PMO manager should be someone that gets things done and makes people's lives easier, that way the role will be well-respected and viewed as a position that adds real value to the organisation.

- Is the method for identifying dependencies effective?
- Do dependencies require approval? What is the approval process?
- When were the project team last trained on dependency management?
- How are the dependency reviews completed?
- What tool are we using to log dependencies?
- How can the process be improved?
- What metrics\reports are currently being circulated?

In addition to the checks above, it's also important to ensure that regular feedback is being provided on the progress of these dependencies to the other required parties. This should also include a way to communicate new and potential dependencies. Another key task is to have a **clearly defined escalation path**. When a project's success is dependent on another team or project, it's imperative to have this escalation route to enable the project to stay on track.

"At a Glance" Metrics

Dependencies are something that are often forgotten about when it comes to reporting, or they are reported through a complicated-looking heat map that doesn't really tell the audience what the dependencies are or when the critical touch points should be. Some examples of these metrics are:

- The number of internal and external dependencies.
- The number of high, medium and low dependencies.
- The number of dependencies without a mitigation plan.
- The details of the dependencies with an impact date due in the next thirty days.

Due to the highly visible nature of external dependencies, the information collated will be used on a number of dashboards and management reports. The aim is for the dependency management process on the programme to be running effectively, enabling the parties requiring information to be kept informed of progress on a regular basis.

Chapter Eight
Change Control

Change control within project management is a formal process used to ensure that changes to a project are introduced in a controlled and coordinated manner. This process supports the identification, documentation, approval or rejection of all changes to a project's baseline.

Definition

Changes to a project are an inevitable part of the project's lifecycle. Therefore, it's important to have a well-defined, well-communicated and robust change control process in place.

> The change control process ensures that each change introduced to the project environment is appropriately defined, evaluated and approved prior to implementation.

Project changes are usually categorised into time, cost, quality, scope, resource or benefits changes. It's important to note that for software or system implementation projects, technical change requests (code or system configuration changes) are out of the scope of the PMO's change control process.

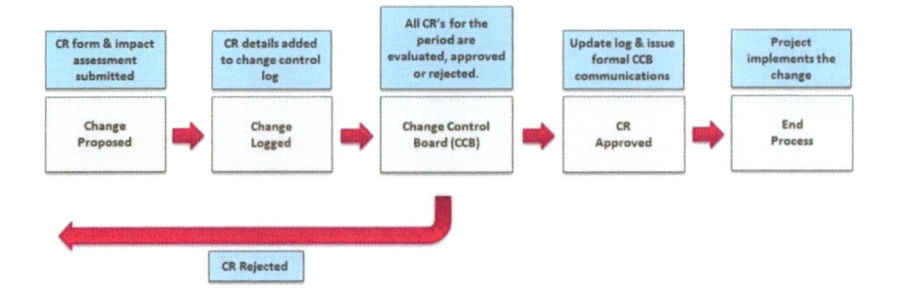

Figure 5. A simplified view – change control process example.

Proposing a Change

The first step in the change control process is for a potential change to be identified. The change control process gives the ability for the customer or anyone in the project team to propose a change to the project. It is important at this initial stage to record the available information about the change in a structured and consistent way.

Change Request (CR) Form

The best way to facilitate this is by using a change request form. This is a clear input document into the process that describes the problem, the reason for the change, including the benefits, and an impact assessment of the areas affected by the change.

Table 11. Change Request Form Field Examples

Field	Definition
Change Request Number\ID	The unique identification number for the change.
Project	The name of the project that owns the change request.
Originator (Raised by:)	The name of individual that raised the change.
Owner	The name of the individual that will own the change request.
Title	A concise but descriptive title for this CR.
Date Raised	The date the change request was raised.
Impact Date	The date on which the change request needs to be implemented.
Description	A clear, non-technical description of the change.
Reason for the Change	A justification for the change. Including details of the impact of not approving this change.
Change Type	The type of change request – Time, Cost, Quality, Scope, Resource or Benefits.

There will usually also be some fields that support the different types of change that can be submitted. For example, a CR for an additional resource will require information such as the duration the resource is required, specific deliverables for the resource during that period, the cost of the resource and, where applicable, a third-party supplier's rate card.

Impact Assessment

The impact assessment should be carried out by the project manager, who needs to take into account the impacts on all aspects of the project.

The following questions should be covered:

- Are there any cost savings or benefits from this change?
- Is there a legal or regulatory reason driving the change?
- What is the estimated cost of the change?
- What are the impacts on the schedule and timeline?
- Are there any extra resources required?
- What are the impacts on other projects and business activities?
- Does this change create any new risks or issues?

Based upon the findings from the impact assessment, the project manager should recommend to the change control board whether to carry out the change.

The Change Control Log (Register)

Once a CR form has been submitted to the PMO, the details of the change need to be recorded for evaluation at the change control board. A change control log is used for this purpose, and the log should contain all of the fields from the CR form listed earlier along with the fields required to document the decision and the next steps following the change control board.

The Change Board (CCB)

The purpose of the change control board is to review, approve, reject or escalate all project or programme changes. This ensures that the impact of any changes has been assessed and decisions have been agreed completely.

The change control board will be chaired by the programme manager, facilitated by the PMO manager, and various change owners for the CRs on the agenda will attend. There will also be a number of other standard CCB attendees, depending on how the project or programme is set up and governed. These can include representatives from finance, vendor management or representatives from the business.

Table 12. Change Control Log Fields (In addition to the CR form fields)

Field	Definition
Change Control Board Date	The date the change request was reviewed by the change control board.
Change Control Board Decision	The outcome of the review by the change control board. Approved, Approved with Action, Deferred with Action, Rejected.
Change Control Board Notes	Any applicable minutes or actions taken from the change control board documenting the decision and next steps.

Closing a Change Request

When the originator confirms the change has been implemented correctly, the CR can then be closed in the change control log. An alternative approach for larger organisations is for a CR to be closed following the close-out of any actions defined by the change control board. For example, when a CR has been formally accepted into the project's scope, a budget uplift has been approved or the extra resource is onboard. It is not always feasible to seek confirmation from the originator of the CR, and therefore closure is agreed by the board after confirmation that the CR is being tracked through other project management controls.

Change Control – Ongoing Management

PMO Analyst Role

As the change control process governs high-visibility changes such as the timeline, budget and the scope of a project or programme, the PMO resources must ensure the process is well-defined, communicated and managed effectively. The PMO analyst must understand all of the steps in the change control process, along with having detailed knowledge about the inputs and outputs of each session.

The PMO analyst should be made aware of all CRs that are submitted for their particular project or programme. They then become the first level of assurance that the CR forms have been completed correctly and the CR is being progressed in line with the defined process.

PMO Manager's Role

Having good content knowledge of the CRs is very important for the PMO manager. They facilitate the change control board and are effectively endorsing that each CR on the agenda is at the right level of detail and is ready for review by the CCB.

PMO managers will track and record the actions and outcomes from the CCB in the change control log. The PMO manager needs to also ensure the loop is closed following the approval of any change requests. For example, has the scope CR been reflected in the latest project schedule? Has the budget CR been reflected in the latest forecast?

"At a Glance" Metrics

Change control metrics often paint a very powerful picture; after all, they are quantifying the variance to the original project baseline across a project's schedule, budget, quality, scope, resource profile or benefits.

Example metrics on change control:

- **The number of each CR type that has been raised against the project.**
  This is particularly important for demonstrating how many times the scope has changed. How many times have we required a change to the budget? How many times have the critical milestones in the schedule been moved?

- **The cumulative value of the CRs with costs associated to them.**
- **The number and type of CRs that are raised in each project phase.**

Chapter Nine
Project Accounting

Definition

The Project accounting is the reporting and progress monitoring of all of the financial aspects of a project. A number of financial reports will be created to track the progress of the project. This enables the monitoring of spend vs budget, spend vs latest forecast, spend against particular purchase orders, performance against the project's benefits profile and many more.

> Project accounting should pull together all of the project's financial data into meaningful reports that enable the project manager and the organisation to make decisions quickly and efficiently.

On a project level, the project manager is informed to make decisions such as addressing overspend or underspend and revise the budgets and forecast accordingly. At an organisational level, project financial reporting allows companies to measure and accurately assess the ROI (return on investment) of individual projects and assists the active management of the portfolio by providing useful financial indicators and metrics.

For the purposes of this book, we are going to concentrate on the project and programme level financial reporting.

Project Finances – Background

The management and control of the project's finances is the responsibility of the project manager. However, the PMO resources are often involved in supporting the project or programme manager with their financial reporting. Therefore, it's important to understand the overall project financial process from requesting a project's budget through to tracking, monitoring and project closure.

The Project Budget

As part of the project approval process, the project budget will have to be reviewed and approved. The project manager will collate the high-level requirements for the project and will then formulate an initial forecast of the project's expenditure. Unless the project can be delivered using "in-house" resources, then the high-level requirements will be sent out to tender where a number of chosen third-party suppliers or partners will review these and provide a quotation for project delivery based on the requirements.

Once the project manager has collated all of this information and has an initial view of the cost of the project, the next steps would be to formally request the allocation of funds for the completion of the project. This would usually require the completion of an investment appraisal form or investment request form and is possibly the first step that would require the support of the PMO resources.

The Investment Appraisal Form

This document contains an overview of the project information, key dates, key resources, project scope and a full breakdown of the financial information to enable the investment board to make an informed decision when reviewing the project.

There are a number of terms (with the definitions below) that require some additional and comprehensive research to fully understand the meaning and the inputs that are required.

Table 13. Project Accounting Topics for Further Review

Term	Definition
Cost Centre	The part of the organisation that will be charged the costs associated with this project.
Capital Expenditure (CAPEX)	The funds used by a company to acquire or upgrade physical assets such as property, hardware or equipment.
Operational Expenditure (OPEX)	The funds that a company spends on an ongoing basis in order to run the business.
Net Present Value (NPV)	An indicator that compares the amount invested in the project to date to the present value of the future income from the project after it has been discounted back to today's value using a specified rate of return.
Internal Rate of Return (IRR)	This is the discount rate at which the net present value of costs of the project equals the net present value of the benefits of the project.

The finance team within the organisation should provide guidance or instruction on how to allocate each of the different expenditure items against CAPEX or OPEX. The PMO resources should familiarise themselves with this "cost treatment guidance", as there are always questions on whether a particular project activity should be treated as CAPEX or OPEX.

The Project Budget Tracker

Once the project budget has been approved, it's imperative that the project manager keeps track and control of it. Supporting the project manager in this activity will often fall to the PMO resources to help update forecasts, track actual spend and provide a view on variances to the forecast.

The project budget, latest forecasts and details of the total expenditure should be tracked and controlled using a project budget tracker. This will either be in the form of a project and portfolio management (PPM) tool or a custom Microsoft Excel spreadsheet.

The project budget tracker should contain the following:

- A month-by-month breakdown of the project budget.
- A month-by-month breakdown of the latest project forecast.
- Project actual spend.
- Variance details – budget vs actual spend, and latest forecast vs actual spend.
- Committed spend – total and breakdown of all purchase orders raised by the project.
- Receipted spend – total and breakdown of the approved payments (receipts) against the purchase orders. This is then matched against a company invoice by the finance team and payment to the company is approved.

It's important to keep in mind that the majority of financial reports will use data from the project budget tracker. Therefore, if these are being newly created the data should be organised in such a way that reports are easily generated.

Project Accounting – Ongoing Tracking and Reporting

PMO Analyst Role

The PMO analyst assigned to the project will often be tasked with assisting the project manager with the tracking, reconciling and reporting of the project's finances. In many cases, the PMO analyst will be assigned after the project is approved, so the initial steps will be to review the project's investment appraisal form and set up a project budget tracker.

Purchase Orders

If purchase orders (POs) are not raised on behalf of the projects by the finance team, the responsibility will fall to the project team. The PMO analyst should fully familiarise themselves with the purchase order system and create a step-by-step guide for use within the project team, demonstrating how to create purchase orders.

This should include details of what information needs to go into each field, cost centre codes that are required in advance and details of the expected attachments. Purchase orders will need to be approved by finance and senior management so it's imperative that steps are put in place to ensure that POs are raised correctly each and every time. Details of the purchase orders should then be logged in the project budget tracker.

Monthly Meetings

A standard set of meetings should be set up between the PMO analyst and the project manager each month to ensure the budget tracker and financial forecasts are up to date and the project's actual spend has been reconciled.

Below is an example of the monthly meetings required. These meetings should be tailored exactly to the organisation's timescales:

Working Day Five – Following the release of the project actual spend report from the finance team, the PMO analyst should reconcile the actual spend against the forecast spend for that particular month. There is also usually a requirement to provide commentary against all variances to the finance team or the programme manager. The PMO analyst can create a draft version of this following their reconciliation of the project actual spend report for the project manager to review.

Working Day Six – The PMO analyst should meet with the project manager to review the variances between the actual spend and the latest forecast alongside the provided variance commentary. The project manager should then revise his future forecast, where applicable, to take into account any unexpected variances.

Working Day Fifteen to Twenty– The PMO analyst should liaise with the project manager to ascertain if the purchase orders forecast to be spent this month can be receipted as planned.

Regular Reviews

In addition to the monthly schedule of finance meetings, there will always be a requirement for additional finance reviews throughout the lifecycle of the project. This could be due to the portfolio amending their budget, the project requesting the next set of finances required from the investment board, or just to align with the organisation's quarterly reporting cycle.

Project financials are always an emotive subject and under constant scrutiny. The PMO can demonstrate real value by knowing the current state of a project's finances inside out.

- When do we need to request the next tranche of finances from the investment board?
- Which POs are being paid this month?
- What was the reason for the variance to the budget or forecast this month?
- What did we overspend on? What did we underspend on?
- What are all of these additional cross-charges for? Can they be reduced?
- Is the project currently over budget?

PMO Manager's Role

The PMO manager will support the programme manager in reporting and tracking the finances at a programme level. The PMO manager will collate the project level finance data each month for review with the programme manager. The same level of checking and reporting is required at programme level as at project level. Variances need to be understood and explained, forecasts need to be amended where required and programme finances need to be reported up to portfolio level.

Process Review

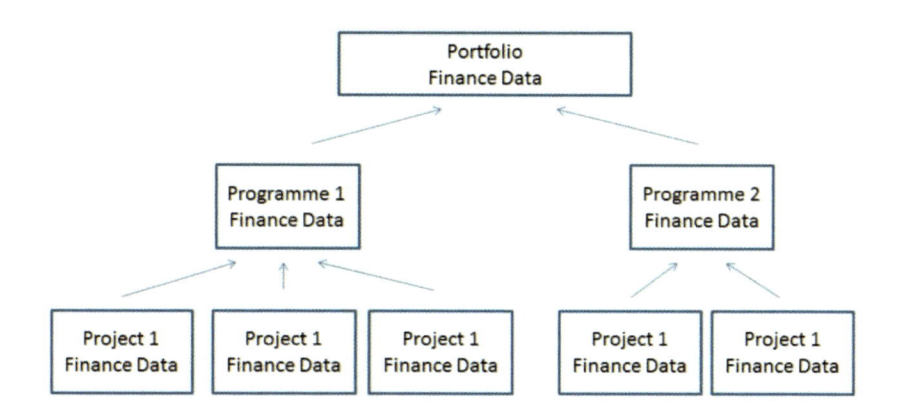

Figure 6. Finance data reporting flow.

The PMO manager should define and optimise the timescales for project and programme financial reporting based upon the reporting requirements set by the portfolio and the release of the project's actual spend report. For example, if the programme finances are reviewed by the portfolio and senior management teams on working day eight of each month, then project level finance data should be submitted to the PMO manager on working day six, meaning the programme review can take place on working day seven prior to the portfolio review.

As part of the process review, the PMO manager should ensure that there is the right level of guidance available to project managers and PMO analysts to walk them through the financial systems and reporting timelines. There are often little-known pitfalls within an organisation that need to be communicated to the project teams in order for them to be avoided. For example, there may be a requirement to complete all of the goods receipting by a particular working day of the month, and any receipts that take place after this deadline will fall into the following month's project actuals. This can have a large and dramatic effect on a project or programme's actual spend and their variances against the forecast.

"At a Glance" Metrics

The subject of the health and status of a project's finances will always have a number of interested, often senior, parties, and will be some of the most widely circulated reports that the PMO produce. The PMO needs to demonstrate a robust reporting process to ensure financial information is current and reports can be pulled together at any time very quickly.

In addition to reporting on a project's financial status, it's important to provide metrics showing a project's financial performance against a defined set of key performance indicators (KPIs).

Some examples of KPIs are:

- % variance to budget each month.
- % variance to budget year to date (YTD).
- % variance to the latest forecast each month.
- % variance to the latest forecast year to date (YTD).
- How has the forecast changed from last month?
- How does that affect the programme budget?
- £s committed but not receipted?

Chapter Ten
Lessons Learned

Definition

The practice of "Lessons Learned" is completing a structured review of a project or a phase of a project in order to learn from the experiences that have gone before and extract any tangible improvements and ideas that can be made to the team's ways of working in the future.

> The process of "Lessons Learned" is the practice of actively learning from the experiences gained from performing a particular project.

Lessons learned should draw on positive experiences, good ideas, cost savings and negative experiences where lessons can be learned from an undesirable outcome.

The large majority of lessons learned workshops take place as part of a project closure phase. However, there is an increasing demand to conduct these reviews at the end of each project phase. This approach is particularly beneficial in global implementations where the same project is performed across a number of countries. That way, actions from the lessons learned sessions can easily be implemented and be in place for the next project.

The Participants

The size and scale of the project will determine if all of the project team, stakeholders and sponsors attend the lessons learned workshop. On larger projects the aim should be to get a good breadth of knowledge across to the attendees and select a sample from the different workstreams, the project management, the business stakeholder and also business sponsorship groups. Try to include people who will provide constructive, valuable insights into the project with an appetite for continuous improvement rather than participants with destructive tendencies. If the numbers of people exceed fifteen to twenty, then it's worth considering holding more than one workshop so that participants have sufficient time to share and learn.

The Process

It's important to note that leadership involvement and commitment to the lessons learned process is critical to the success of the process and embedding a culture of continuous improvement on the project or programme. An effective lessons learned process requires a well-defined and disciplined procedure that is endorsed by the leadership team and is mandatory for the project team to follow. Unfortunately, if there is little appetite from the leadership team to learn from their mistakes, it is unlikely that the lessons learned process will succeed.

Once the frequency of the lessons learned workshops has been decided, they should then be embedded into the delivery methodology of the project and used to foster an environment of continuous improvement. Project team members should know and be encouraged to record improved ways of working and to think about the root cause of a particular problem with a view to solving it.

It's natural to want to improve and to work in a more efficient way. Therefore, lessons learned should be pitched as a valuable opportunity to promote better ways of working. If the project team feel their views are being listened too and actual change is demonstrated, then participation at the lessons learned workshops will be much greater.

Identification → Validation → Action

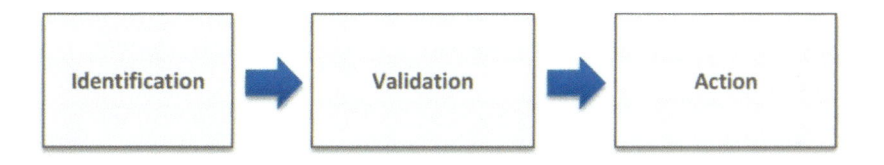

Figure 7. A simplified view – lessons learned process.

Identification

The identification stage of lessons learned is a two-step process: a well-constructed email questionnaire followed by a lessons learned workshop. The questionnaire should be communicated to the project team and stakeholders approximately one month in advance of the lessons learned workshop; this encourages the start of the lessons learned thought process. The questionnaire should be simple but also accompanied by a well-drafted communication detailing the purpose, the process and the added value of the lessons learned process.

The Lessons Learned Workshop

A lessons learned workshop can be one of the more difficult sessions to facilitate, so it's even more important that this is planned correctly and the meeting ground rules are communicated. The tone of the meeting should be constructive, with the mindset to continuously improve, not to blame members of the team. The difficulty is maintaining the balance of focus whilst allowing the freedom to share ideas and debate solutions. Placing an emphasis on working towards a solution instead of dwelling on the problems will facilitate a more productive session.

Although there are no set of "right" questions to ask throughout the workshop, I've included some examples to assist with setting the agenda. The workshop can be split by project phase to help target specific thoughts and also segregate the workshop into time slots to ensure an end-to-end view of the project is reviewed.

Sample Lessons Learned Questions

1. What worked well?
2. What would you do differently?
3. What change requests were applied to the project? Scope, budget, resources or schedule? What were the root causes of these? Could they have been avoided?
4. How was the project planned? How was the project schedule estimated? How were the project resources planned?
5. How were project risks identified, managed, and resolved?
6. What processes were easy to use or effective?
7. What processes were difficult to understand or ineffective?
8. What project events weren't anticipated?

It's important to pursue a discussion topic through to the identification of a root cause; unless the true root cause is understood, it's difficult to assign ownership of any resulting action.

The "5 Whys" is a useful technique to drive a conversation through to a root cause:

Five Whys Example[1]

> The vehicle will not start. (The problem.)
> Why? – The battery is dead. (First why.)
> Why? – The alternator is not functioning. (Second why.)
> Why? – The alternator belt has broken. (Third why.)
> Why? – The alternator belt was well beyond its useful service life and not replaced. (Fourth why.)

Why? – The vehicle was not maintained according to the recommended service schedule. (Fifth why – a root cause.)

The Lessons Learned Log

Each of the proposed lessons learned, along with the root cause and subsequent action plan, should be documented in a lessons learned log. This will be used to track the items identified until they have been mitigated to an acceptable level.

---

[1] http://en.wikipedia.org/wiki/5_Whys

LESSONS LEARNED LOG						
ID	Date Identified	Owner	Potential Lesson	Root Cause	Action Plan	Follow Up Required?

Project Name:
Project Manager:
Project Description:

Figure 8. Lessons learned log example.

Validation

Once the potential lessons have been identified, they require a level of validation before being accepted and tracked as actions for the applicable project team member. If there was a good level of attendance at the lessons learned workshop, then the validation of each of the lessons may also have taken place in that session. However, there may be a requirement for a subject matter expert to review the proposed lesson and advised root cause to validate it and advise an appropriate course of action.

Action

In a similar way to logging risks, issues or dependencies, an owner should be assigned to each lesson learned that will own the action plan to ensure the lesson is truly learned and mitigated for future projects. The owner will confirm and accept the mitigation or action plan and provide a target completion date.

Lessons Learned – Ongoing Management

As part of the project closure process, the project manager will ensure all lessons have an owner and the mitigation action plan has been accepted, along with a target completion date and communication of how these lessons will be tracked after the project has been closed. The owners should be leads from an applicable business unit or workstreams that can implement any mitigating actions after the project team has been disbanded.

PMO Analyst Role

The PMO resources play a big role in the facilitation and administration of the lessons learned workshop and resulting log. They also usually have a vested interest in lessons learned as the work of the PMO continues after the project has been closed down, and therefore it's beneficial to ensure that the lessons learned action plans have been addressed.

The PMO analyst should ensure that the lessons learned process is communicated and understood by the proposed attendees. Using the good practices from the earlier meeting facilitation chapter, the invites, agenda and initial lessons learned questionnaire should be sent out well in advance.

The PMO analyst will log the proposed lessons, along with owners, details of the root cause discussions and any action plans or next steps that are highlighted.

PMO Manager Role

The PMO manager, or project manager, will facilitate the workshop, initially setting the scene, reiterating the purpose of the session and covering the ground rules and behaviours that are expected.

Each of the discussion topics should be sufficiently reviewed to highlight the root cause alongside an agreed owner and action plan.

One of the most important aspects to the lessons learned process is following through on the findings and ensuring the agreed actions actually take place. Due to the incredibly busy project environment, the project team are almost always scheduled immediately to their next assignment following the closure of the project, therefore getting the lessons learned actions completed is always challenging. The most effective method of ensuring these actions are completed is to log the actions to be reviewed at the next project's team meetings or logging risks that need to be mitigated by the next project team.

If the actions agreed from the lessons learned session do not have a home in the future where they will be managed through to completion, the likelihood is that they will be filed away and never addressed.

The PMO manager working at programme level can add real value to the programme by following through on these actions and realising tangible improvements across the programme.

Chapter Eleven
Document Version Control

Version control should be utilised for all PMO documentation that is likely to be revised or redrafted, and a record is required to be kept of how the document has changed over time. Quite often, organisations will already have a version control system that can simply be applied by the PMO. It's important for the PMO to train and communicate the version control system so that it is applied consistently across the projects and programmes.

The benefits of using version control are:

- Version history is tracked to understand how a document was changed and developed.
- The team can be confident they are reading the most up-to-date version of a document.
- Old or redundant versions can be deleted.
- Versions are tracked and dated so the team can understand when a document was approved and came into force.

Static Documents

Static documents are changed infrequently, such as process documentation or charters. For static documents, the version should be stated as part of the document name. For example:

Draft Versions
"PMO Charter v0.1.doc" → "PMO Charter v0.2.doc" → "PMO Charter v0.3.doc" etc.

<u>Finalised Approved Version</u>

"PMO Charter v1.0.doc"

<u>Subsequent Amendments to the Approved Version</u>

"PMO Charter v1.1.doc" → "PMO Charter v1.2.doc" → "PMO Charter v1.3.doc" etc.

<u>Approved Version Following a Major Update</u>

"PMO Charter v2.0.doc"

Version Control Tables

Static documents will require a version control table which should be inserted at the beginning of the document. This is particularly important in legal and regulatory documents that require a clear audit trail of document changes.

Table 14. Version Control Table Example

Version	Date	Author	Changes
0.1	DD/MM/YY	M.Readman	-
0.2	DD/MM/YY	M.Readman	Feedback from PMO team included
0.3	DD/MM/YY	M.Readman	Feedback from management team included
1	DD/MM/YY	M.Readman	Approved version

Dynamic Documents

Dynamic documents are changed frequently and are tracked through the inclusion of the date within the document name. Examples of dynamic documents would be risk logs or action logs.

"PMO Risk Log v05122014" or "PMO Risk Log v05-12-2014"

For documents that require more frequent updates than daily, then initials can be included in the document name. For example:

"PMO Risk Log vMR051214" or "PMO Risk Log vMR05-12-2014"

Chapter Twelve
Final Thoughts

There will never be hard and fast rules dictating that all PMOs should be the same in every organisation. The PMO should be fluid and fit around the requirements of the PMO sponsor and senior management. They will input to the type of PMO that is required and the areas of governance that they would like to be under the PMO's control.

Throughout this book I have described the different PMO controls in terms of best practice and rigid governance. Once you understand the controls at this level, it's very easy to adapt them to the requirements of the organisation. A far higher level of governance is required for industries such as banking, telecoms or pharmaceuticals, with medium or small to medium-sized businesses generally preferring a less stringent approach. If your organisation currently has a light touch PMO, there are usually occasions where you are asked to tighten up certain controls due to problems that have arisen. This is always far easier to tackle if you have previous experience of working in a PMO that tightly governs their processes.

PMO resources should be open-minded to different ways of working and be optimistic when it comes to change but should always keep in mind the best and proven practices for governing the PMO.

What do I look for when recruiting PMO resources?

After reading this book you will have noticed some common themes that are less specific to the PMO controls and more about the personality and mindset required to have a successful career in the PMO. In my opinion, these would be valuable attributes to anyone in any career but they are traits that I particularly look out for when recruiting PMO staff.

Drive

I like to have a team that are driven, thirsty for knowledge and have an active interest in progressing and understanding the role on the next step of the career path. I always encourage the team to ask questions. It's normal for someone to have strengths and weaknesses, but the weaknesses should always be viewed as areas of opportunity to improve and not areas to shy away from. Succession planning is very important to me, and ensuring a team dynamic where everyone is working towards their next career move creates a fantastic working environment with a well-motivated workforce.

Passion

The PMO is all about the details: noticing changes from week to week, quality checking material to ensure it's compliant with the process, and also building relationships across the business. A good attention to detail and a passion for what you do are "must-haves" in the PMO. Senior management base their decisions on accurate information. If you can provide valuable independent insights into how the projects are performing and possible problems before they arise, then you will be demonstrating the behaviours of a high-performing team member.

Content Knowledge

Understanding the role of the PMO within the organisation and also the full content of your role within the PMO is very important. Any or all of the PMO controls that have been covered could be within your remit when taking up a new role, therefore, it's imperative that you understand each of them in full detail. The most respected people in any organisation are those who understand fully what they are talking about and when questioned give the right answer every time. The larger the organisation the more valuable this becomes. These processes are rarely subject to a full review. Instead, steps are added as required until usually the process becomes quite unwieldy. By tracing back through the antiquated and intricate process steps to understand the full flow and the key parties involved, you will understand the process from end to end, you will be able to offer guidance on the existing process to other parties and also offer insight on how the process can be improved.

Loyalty

Projects and programmes are unpredictable environments. There will always be occasions where you are required to "go the extra mile" and demonstrate commitment to the role. I've had many late nights through my career, finalising executive steering reports or problem-solving with senior management. As long as these late nights don't become an everyday occurrence, they should be embraced and viewed as an opportunity to improve the ways of working in the future.

The PMO now has a well-defined and prosperous career path, taking you up to director level within some of the largest companies in the world. Gaining a firm grounding in governance, delivery and best practice will give you the characteristics to go on and become a very well-respected senior manager. The most effective leaders I've worked for are those that are well organised and have the information flows set up to know exactly what they need to know, every time they need it.

Be mindful of these best practices, learn behaviours from the leaders that you respect, always set the highest of standards, and you will go very far in your PMO career.

Printed in Great Britain
by Amazon